Who Is This King Of Glory?

Crystal Trower

ISBN: 978-1-60383-293-9

Published by:
Holy Fire Publishing
717 Old Trolley Rd.
Atten: Suite 6, Publishing Unit #116
Summerville, SC 29485

www.ChristianPublish.com

Cover Design: Jay Cookingham

Edited by: Tracy Ruckman Freelance Editor www.WriteIntegrity.com

Printed in the United States of America and the United Kingdom

Half Price Books
1835 Forms Drive
Carrollton, TX 75006
OFS OrderID 38623999

Thank you for your order, Main Address!

Thank you for shopping with Half Price Books! Please contact service116@hpb.com. if you have any questions, comments or concerns about your order (113-5971187-8669806)

Visit our stores to sell your books, music, movies games for cash.

SKU	ISBN/UPC	Title & Author/Artist	Shelf ID	Qty	OrderSKU
S465257134	9781603832939	Who Is This King Of Glory? Trower, Crystal	REL 21.1	1	

SHIPPED STANDARD TO:
Main Address
800 Avondale Ave
1033648-1-0325
Grandview Heights OH 43212
zypxchqnwm9p8bz@marketplace.amazon.com

ORDER# **113-5971187-8669806**
AmazonMarketplaceUS

This study is dedicated to my mother.

Thank you for introducing me to Jesus. I am so blessed to have been raised in a Christian home under the influence of a godly woman. I remember seeing you so often with a cup of coffee in hand and a Bible in your lap. Thank you for being such a wonderful Christ-follower. You inspired me to seek Jesus for myself.

Thank you for pointing me toward the Cross.

"Lift up your heads, O you gates;

Be lifted up, you ancient doors,

That the King of Glory may come in.

Who is this King of Glory?

The Lord strong and mighty,

The Lord mighty in battle.

Lift up your heads, O you gates;

Lift them up, you ancient doors,

That the King of glory may come in.

Who is He, this King of glory?

The Lord Almighty—

he is the King of glory."

Psalm 24:7-10 NIV

TABLE OF CONTENTS

Introduction:

I can't wait to start this study with you. This study has been on my mind for some time. God placed it there awhile ago and had me wait for His timing to put it into writing. This is His timing and I am so excited to share what He has laid on my heart with you. I started putting this study on paper shortly after God spoke to me in a Sunday service at my church. I was sitting there just taking in the message when the pastor said the words "crystal clear." I didn't hear his words right after that, but I did hear my Lord's Words to me. He spoke to my heart ..."Did you hear that? Crystal clear? "Clear" is the meaning of your name. I have a job for you ... to make Me "clear" to other people ... to tell them Who I really Am ... not Who they think I Am, but Who I really Am." That's where this study comes from . . . from a Word spoken to my heart from my Lord. I want to introduce you to Jesus. I can't wait for you to meet Him. Let's join hands and run to see my Friend

WEEK ONE:

CREATOR OF ALL THINGS

"For by him all things were created: things in heaven and on earth, visible and invisible, whether thrones or powers or rulers or authorities; all things were created by him and for him."

Colossians 1:16

DAY ONE: GOD THE SON

DAY TWO: SOMETHING FROM NOTHING

DAY THREE: MARVELOUS CREATION

DAY FOUR: MOST PRECIOUS CREATION

DAY FIVE: THE SIGNIFICANT OTHERS

DAY ONE: GOD THE SON

We are going to dive right in today and clear up a huge misconception that many people have about Jesus Christ. I will just go ahead and say the words that offend so many **... Jesus is God**. I won't start off by "beating around the bush". Scripture is very clear that this statement is true. Let's prove it together:

Look up the following Scriptures and fill in the blanks:

John 1:1 "In the beginning was the Word, and the Word was ________ God, and the Word _______ God."

Hebrews 1:3 "The Son is the _________ of God's glory and the exact _____________ of his Being, sustaining all things by his powerful ______."

John 14:7, 9b "If you really knew me, you would know my _________ as well. From now on, you do know him and have _______ him ... Anyone who has seen _____ has seen the _________."

Exodus 3:14 "God said to Moses, '... This is what you are to say to the Israelites: ___ _____ has sent me to you.'"

John 8:58 "'I tell you the truth,' Jesus answered, 'before Abraham was born, ___ _____.'"

Did you see what I saw in these verses? Let me give it to you in the form of a simple mathematical equation. (My favorite subject in school was Math).

Think back to your school days ... if a=b and b=c then a=c

Let a=Jesus Let b=The Father Let c=God

You fill in the equation: If (a)________=(b)_________ and (b)_________=(c)_________ then (a)_________=(c)__________

Look at your conclusion. Is it becoming crystal clear to you?

If you think about it, everyone has an opinion of Jesus. There is no "neutral" ground when it comes to His Name. Think of all the controversy that can be stirred up or the uncomfortable silence that is brought on at the mere mention of the Name of Jesus.

Some get angry … some get excited … some get scared … some get resentful … some get curious … some get hopeful … some get tearful … everyone feels something at the mention of His Name.

What do you "feel" at the mention of Jesus' Name?______________________________

During the days that Jesus walked on this earth, there were many opinions of who He really was.

Read Matthew 16:13-14.

Who did people say that He was?____

Who do you say that He is? ____

____

____

I think we should end on that note for today. Don't worry if you had trouble filling in the last question. Take a few minutes to pray and ask Christ to reveal Himself to you a little more each day through this study as you spend time in His Word. He wants to be known. He already knows you, take some time to get to know Him … you are going to love Him.

DAY TWO: SOMETHING FROM NOTHING

Do you know some of the words I hate to hear the most? "Mom, I have a project to do for school." The only words that could make this statement any worse are "due tomorrow." I don't know about you, but I don't get very excited about school projects, especially the ones that require any kind of creativity. The student's project really ends up being the parent's project. Please don't be offended if you are a teacher. It's almost like we are expected to create something out of nothing. You moms know what I mean. You can do a lot of things with a shoebox, but let's be honest, you can't really make a miracle happen.

Once, my oldest son, who was in 6th or 7th grade at the time, had to build Noah's Ark out of Triscuits. And it had to be to scale. I threw my hands up with that one and did the only thing I knew to do … I left it for my husband to finish. I think my son got a "C" on that project. It's funny as I look back on all the school projects I have done (I mean "helped with" for all you teachers) with each child (I have three), the projects have become less elaborate and less creative. By the time my third child started having projects to do, our finished products have consisted of stick figures, paper sacks, and plain white poster board. I am encouraged by the fact that I only have two more years of the Science Fair to go.

Where am I going with this? All that, to say that Jesus Christ is Creator of All Things. Can you imagine? I have trouble decorating a shoebox. He created the universe just by speaking. I can talk all day to a shoebox, but it's not going to make something out of itself. Jesus spoke and the world came into being. Our minds just cannot grasp it.

Let's look at Creation according to Genesis. Read Genesis Chapter 1.

What did God create on:

Day One?____

Day Two?____

Day Three?____

Day Four? ____

Day Five?____

Day Six?____

Look at verses 3, 6, 9, 14, 20, 24, and 26.

What three words do these verses have in common? "________ _______

________"

Jesus just spoke and things happened. "And God said …." (Remember our equation from Day One?)

Let me share with you some of the most impressive verses in all of Scripture.

Fill in the blanks:

Psalm 33:6-9 "By the _______ of the Lord were the heavens made, their starry host by the __________ of his mouth. He __________ the waters of the sea into jars; he puts the deep into storehouses. Let all the earth _______ the Lord; Let all the people of the world _________ him. For he _________, and it came to be; he _______________, and it stood firm."

Psalm 74:15-17 "It was you who _________ up springs and streams; you __________ up the ever flowing rivers. The ______ is yours, and yours is also the _________; you established the ______ and _________. It was you who set all the __________________ of the earth; you made both __________ and ____________."

Psalm 147:16-18 "He spreads the ________ like wool and scatters the _________ like ashes. He hurls down his _________ like pebbles. Who can withstand his icy blast? He sends his ________ and melts them; he stirs up his _____________ and the waters flow."

WHO is This?

Do you have goose bumps? I can't help but get them when I read those verses. Do you know what amazes me the most when I read these Scriptures? Remember yesterday, when I said that Jesus wants to be known? He wants us to know Him. To know Him personally. Think about that for a minute. The Creator of the entire universe wants you to know Him. Have you ever felt kind of "cool" because you knew someone important? I've felt a little high and mighty when we haven't had to wait at some particular restaurants because we know the owners. Imagine being friends with the Owner of the universe. That's what He wants … to be your Friend.

Let's end today with this thought:

Write in your own words what you think it means to be a "friend" to someone____

____

____

____

If you haven't already, will you start a friendship with Him today? ________________

____

If you already know Him as Friend, how has He shown His friendship to you lately?

____

____

DAY THREE: MARVELOUS CREATION

Today is going to look a little different than our other study days. We're going on a field trip. Don't worry, I'm not talking about the kind where you have to tour the post office with 100 first graders. I'm talking about a field trip with Jesus. Just you and Him. It sure beats the post office trip. You can actually enjoy some peace and quiet with Him.

Here's what I want us to do:

Use our study time today to marvel at His creation. How often do you really take time to do this? If you're like me, the only time I really stop and "marvel" is when I'm at the beach, when I actually have time to just sit and take in the beach scenery. I want us to get outside if possible … yes, even if it's cold. Just bundle up and get outdoors. Go to the park, talk a walk around your neighborhood, (I guess I'll let a drive around the block count as well), as long as you can see the outdoors. If you are at home with little ones, maybe slip into the back yard for a few minutes while they nap (naptime is sacred.) Whatever you have to do to get outdoors for a little while with Jesus, as the saying goes … "just do it."

Spend some time just marveling at His creation. Talk with Him about it. Tell Him what impresses you. Ask Him why on earth He created bugs? Whatever comes to mind, just talk to Him about it. It will surprise you, the things you might notice that you hadn't before.

When you come back from your field trip, write down your thoughts on His marvelous creation.

I'll give you a whole page to write, just in case . . .

WHO is This?

DAY FOUR: MOST PRECIOUS CREATION

I hope you enjoyed your field trip with Jesus yesterday. Today, we'll stay inside and study, unless it's gorgeous outside where you are, then be my guest, take your Bible and notebook outside and let's get started.

Today, we're going to look at His Most Precious Creation. I'll give you one guess as to what (or should I say 'who') it is. If you need a hint, let's look at Genesis 1 again.

Read Genesis 1:26-27.

What (or Who) was His final creation on the Sixth Day? ____________

His most precious creation is **YOU**. Let that sink in for a minute…

Put your name in the blank:

I, ______________, am His most precious creation.

Doesn't that sound so sweet with your name in the blank? I don't know about you, but I don't always feel special. Especially on the days when I've been busy with the kids all day (which is everyday) and I haven't even had time to make myself look presentable. You know the days I'm talking about, those when you hope nobody stops by your house because you and the house are both a mess. Most of us don't go around feeling special all the time, but guess what? We are. You are. Whether we feel like it or even look like it, we are. I know SomeOne who thinks you are the "most specialist" (as my kids used to say). Remember in elementary school when you liked a certain boy, you would send your friend to find out what he thought about you, and she would come back with a report? Well, I have a good report for you from this Guy named Jesus. Let me tell you what He said about you.

Look up the following Scriptures and fill in the blanks:

Song of Songs 2:14 "…show Me your face, let Me hear your __________; for your voice is __________, and your face is ____________."

WHO is This?

Song of Songs 4:9a "You have stolen My __________, My sister, My bride; you have stolen My ___________ . . ."

Song of Songs 4:7 "All ___________you are, My darling; there is no ______ in you."

I was going to send Him a note that said "Do you like (your name)?" Circle "yes" or "no." But you already know the answer after looking up those scriptures. The answer is "Yes." He not only likes you, He loves you. He thinks you are beautiful. You are so precious to Him. I told you that you were going to like this Guy named Jesus.

How does it feel to know that the Creator of the universe adores you?

____

____

____

Let's end today in prayer. Spend some time talking with Him, let Him show you in the coming weeks how special you are to Him.

DAY FIVE: THE SIGNIFICANT OTHERS

Did you enjoy letting Jesus lavish you with compliments yesterday? I know I did. There's nothing that can brighten your day like a good compliment. Especially the "hair" compliments, or the "you look like you've lost weight" compliments. We all love a good compliment. If we get enough of them, we start to feel pretty good about ourselves.

When I was little, I would visit a side of the family I didn't get to see very much. I was the grandchild they didn't get to see very often, and boy, was I treated special. I thought I hung the moon after I returned from a visit there. (But we already learned a couple of days ago Who really hung the moon.) I liked going there because everyone made over me the whole time I was there. I got special treatment. I could pretty much get away with anything while I was there or ask for anything and usually get it. They would even do special grocery shopping before I got there to make sure they had all the stuff I liked. When I came home, my mom had to kindly remind me that I was back in the real world and it wasn't all about me.

After yesterday's study, I thought you and I might start thinking it's all about us after reveling in all those compliments. The neat thing about Jesus is that He not only shows us how special we are to Him, but at the same time, allows us to see others through His Eyes. Boy, does this change our view of the world. I don't know about you, but I can always use a good look through Jesus' eyes at those around me. How easily I forget to show compassion to those around me. How quickly I forget to love those around me.

Let's look at what Jesus says about those around us.

Answer the questions using the following Scriptures:

Who does Jesus want to be saved?____________________ 1 Timothy 2:3-4

Does this include **everyone** that comes across my path?

Circle One: a) Yes b) No c) Only the Nice Ones

WHO is This?

It's tempting to circle answer "c," isn't it? Surely, Jesus doesn't want to save the person that cuts you off on the road ... or the person who goes through the "express" check-out lane with more than the appropriate amount of items ... or, surely not, the neighbor that gets mad when your kids step one foot on his grass. Surely, Jesus didn't mean these people when He said "all men," did He?

When our family first moved to the house we now live in, we didn't really make a good impression on one particular neighbor. You see, we threw a big birthday party for our ten-year-old son out in our backyard one summer evening. I was so excited because I had rented one of those huge, bouncy slides that reach halfway to heaven. When I rented it, I wasn't really thinking about it making much noise, other than the screaming children that would be sliding down it. I didn't realize it had a "motor" that ran the entire time it was set up ... a "motor" that sounded like someone holding a pressure washer right next to your ear. We rented this slide for four hours, by the way. Our neighbors had to listen to this motor for 4 hours, which was very unpleasant if any of them tried to sit on their porches that evening. Long story short ... we got a phone call halfway through the party. (They weren't complimenting us on a well-thrown event.) I was pretty mad at first. Didn't they know we were doing it for the kids? Didn't they know it was just for one evening? They could've gone out to dinner during our party if they didn't want to hear the noise, couldn't they? I ranted and raved to my husband about this complaint for a few days (probably seemed like weeks to him.) One morning, I was sitting on my back porch with my coffee and my Bible, talking to the Lord, enjoying myself, when all of the sudden God spoke to my heart and said "Love your neighbor." I started to feel a little guilty for how I had reacted over those past few days so I responded to the Lord "Ok, I won't be mad at that particular neighbor anymore. I'll just let it go." I sensed the words again ..."Love your neighbor." I thought maybe the Lord didn't hear me so I repeated myself ... "Ok, Lord, I said I won't be mad anymore, and I'm sorry for how I acted." But He wasn't satisfied with that. "Loving your neighbor isn't just not being mad at them; it's intentionally showing love to them by your actions." Where was He going with this? I definitely did not want to do something nice for my neighbor. I had already decided I was just going to avoid that person from now on, you know, look the other way when they wave at me, that kind of thing. Was God really asking me to **do** something nice for them? To show love to them that I didn't feel in my heart?

He most certainly was. I didn't like it too much, but I went to the bakery and picked up some cookies, walked to their house, knocked on the door, gave them the cookies with an apology about disturbing the neighborhood that night of the party. I think they were taken aback by the gesture. I know I was, because I didn't really mean it, but as I walked home that day from their house, God did something in my heart. He was showing me what it really means to love my neighbor. It was a hard lesson, but as I look back, my heart is softened toward that neighbor. I'm thankful for that "complaint" phone call because God used it to do a work in my heart.

What about you? Does He need to do a work in your heart when it comes to loving your neighbor? Let's look at some scriptures.

Matthew 19:19 We are to love our ________________ as ourselves.

Romans 15:2 Each of us should please our ____________________.

Psalm 15:3 We are to do our _________________ no harm.

Do you see the pattern here? We are to actively love our "neighbor" . . . those all around us.

Let's end today with this:

Pray and ask the Lord to show you someone whom you need to show love to this week. Write that person's name here: ______________________

You never know what He might do in **your** heart as you show love to someone else.

WEEK TWO:

BABY IN A MANGER

"While they were there, the time came for the baby to be born, and she gave birth to her firstborn, a son. She wrapped him in cloths and placed him in a manger, because there was no room for them in the inn."

Luke 2:6-7

DAY ONE: GIVING IT ALL UP

DAY TWO: GROWING UP

DAY THREE: DAY TO DAY

DAY FOUR: PART OF THE FAMILY

DAY FIVE: BEEN THERE, DONE THAT

DAY ONE: GIVING IT ALL UP

Last week, we focused on Christ's Deity. Remember our mathematical equation? We proved it … Jesus is God. This week, we are going to focus on something that I think is even harder to wrap our minds around—Jesus' Humanity. Jesus is fully God, yet He became fully human and walked on this earth in the flesh. It's hard to imagine, isn't it? Just think if He had chosen our day and time to walk on this earth in the flesh … imagine walking through the mall and seeing Jesus shopping for shoes. I wonder what kind He would pick out? We have a lot more choices than just those sandals He wore back then. I wonder if He would pay the outrageous prices for certain tennis shoes that make you run faster and jump higher. Who knows? It's hard to think about the Creator of the universe walking around among His Creation. But that is exactly what He did. What blows my mind, is what He gave up so He could become a man and walk among His children.

Have you ever had to give up anything? Like downsizing to a smaller house? Or maybe getting a smaller car that is better on gas? Or maybe you have gone through a job loss where you and your family have had to change your entire lifestyle. I don't know about you, but I get pretty comfortable with the "things" in my life. My husband is always on me about cleaning out my "side" of the closet. His side is a lot neater than mine (not because he is a neater person than I am, but because he has a lot less stuff than I do.) My side of the closet looks like all the racks might just pull away from the wall at any minute. (I really am nervous about that. I don't want to walk in one day to find the walls caved in on my side.) I don't like to part with any of my clothes or shoes. Even the ones I haven't worn in years. I always remind my husband that we could have another Great Depression and he will be glad I saved my stuff because he might have to wear some of it. Or we might be here during the Great Tribulation (some say that believers will have to live during that time, others say believers will already be in heaven. I vote for the latter.) Just in case, I don't want to be without enough clothing when things go haywire.

All that to say that I don't like to give stuff up. I like my stuff. Do you know what Jesus gave up for you? For you to be able to be friends with Him?

Look up the following verses and write some things that Jesus gave up for you?

Hebrews 2:9-14, 5:7-10, 7:26-28, 10:5-10 Isaiah 52:13-15, 53:1-12

____

____

____

Are you overwhelmed by His sacrifice for you? You must be important for Him to give up all that for you. Why don't you spend the rest of your study time pondering what He gave up for you? His seat in heaven, His "hanging out" with the angels, His taking on a human body limited by time and space, His life. Just to name a few.

Spend some time in prayer thanking Him for the sacrifice He made just so He could call you His friend.

Write whatever He speaks to your heart:

____

____

____

DAY TWO: GROWING UP

I wonder what it would have been like to grow up with Jesus, like if you or I had been part of His earthly family way back when, maybe His sister or something. Would you have been jealous because you were always the one in trouble and never Jesus? I always tease my sister and remind her that she was always the one who got in trouble when we were kids. Then she reminds me that we switched places when we became teenagers and I was the one always in trouble. I wonder if His siblings teased Him about being Mr. Perfect … Mama's Boy … Goody Two Shoes. Since He never sinned, I guess He never got in a fistfight with any of them.

I wish I could say the same. The one and only "physical" fight my sister and I got into was when we were teenagers. It was over something really important—clothes. I guess you wouldn't really call it a fist fight, but more like a "hair-pulling" fight. We were in the car with my mom, pulling into my "papaw's" driveway, stopping in for a visit. My sister and I argued all the way there over who was going to get to wear a certain outfit (we were both the same size). Mom goes on in the house and we were lagging behind. I got out of the car and started walking up the hill to the house and suddenly, someone (my sister.) jerks me back down the hill by my hair. Needless to say, I wasn't Mrs. Perfect and I fought back. We were hair pulling, rolling down the hill on my "papaw's" front lawn. He is the one who saw us first out the window. He told my mom, "the girls sure are fighting out there." My mom said, "Yes … they argued all the way here." Then she looked out the window. I think she almost had a heart attack right there. She had never had to break up a physical fight before. (There were no boys in our family … except Dad.) She still tells that story to this day with a look of horror on her face.

My sister and I are both adults now. It's good to be a "grown-up," but do you ever feel like you still have some growing to do? I am in my late 30's now so I probably won't get any taller … maybe "fuller." So I guess I'm full grown physically, but definitely not spiritually. I still have a lot of growing up to do. Don't we all? The great thing is that we have SomeOne to help us, to come along side us, to cheer us on, to pick us up when we fall, to correct us when we falter, to strengthen us when we are weak, to sit with us and teach us the meaning of His Word. What an amazing Friend we have in Jesus.

Look up the following Scriptures and choose your answers to the following statements:

True or False Christ waits until we "clean ourselves up" before being willing to have a relationship with us. (Romans 5:8)

True or False Christ wants to continually remind us of all the things we have done wrong. (Isaiah 43:25)

True or False Jesus wants to "kick us" when we're down. (John 3:17)

True or False Jesus gets mad when we mess up. (Psalm 103:14)

True or False Jesus wants to keep us guessing. (James 1:5)

True or False Jesus doesn't want us to really know Him. (Hebrews 8:11)

These statements might have seemed a little silly; all the answers were a great big "FALSE." But sometimes we have wrong notions in our heads about who this Jesus really is. Maybe from something we read that painted a false picture of Him, or something a well-meaning pastor said that painted a distorted picture as well, or even what our parents taught us was a little skewed. I don't know your background, but we all have had life experiences that have shaped our image of Christ into something not entirely true.

I know that growing up, especially for girls, we tend to compare our Heavenly Father to our earthly father. We tend to assign traits to Him that our earthly father demonstrated to us. I love my earthly father (or actually 'fathers,' because I have a dad and a step-dad). I love my 'dads,' but neither of them are perfect. They didn't always do the right thing or treat me the right way. They always loved me growing up, but they are flawed sinners just like you and me. I cannot compare my Jesus to my earthly fathers. He is The Perfect Father. He knows me perfectly. He does the perfect things to help me grow. He has perfect timing, perfect comfort, perfect answers for me, and perfect lessons for me to learn. I am so thankful to have a Perfect Father to "grow up" with. How about you? Do you need Him to do something "perfect" in your life today? Spend some time talking with Him about it and write your thoughts:

DAY THREE: DAY TO DAY

How is your day-to-day life? Is it exciting? Monotonous? Thrilling? Tiring? Boring? Maybe all of the above? I bet that most of us could say we could use a little more excitement in our lives. A little more thrill. I don't know about you, but I don't get "thrilled" about doing laundry, or ecstatic over going to the grocery, or even celebrate while I help the kids with homework. (I have already told you about my attitude toward school projects.) If you aren't always walking around the house, your job, etc., singing the "Hallelujah Chorus," then you are probably in the norm. Most of us aren't always excited about our day-to-day routines. But I know SomeOne Who wants to add a little more excitement to your life, wants to give you a little more "bounce" in your step, a little more "thrill" to your day. His name is Jesus. You know, the Guy we've been talking about the last several days … Jesus.

Do you know how He wants to do this? By giving you a "greater perspective" on your day-to-day living. His perspective. Life is all about perspective, isn't it? It reminds me of a funny movie where the guy asks the girl what his chances are of dating her. She answers, "one in a million." He gets this great big smile on his face and says, "So you're saying there is a chance." It's all in our perspective. God wants to give us His perspective on our daily lives. This changes everything. Let's check out His perspective:

Fill in the blanks:

2 Corinthians 4:16 "Therefore, we do not lose heart. Though outwardly we are wasting away, but ______________ we are being renewed _____ by ______."

2 Corinthians 4:17 "For our light and ____________ troubles are achieving for us an ___________ glory that far outweighs them all."

2 Corinthians 4:18 "So we fix our eyes not on what is ________, but on what is _________. For what is seen is ____________, but what is unseen is ______________."

WHO is This?

Ephesians 6:7-8 "Serve ____________, as if you were serving the _______, not men, because you know that the Lord will ___________ everyone for whatever good he does."

Does this add a little "bounce" to your step?

List some of your daily "activities" (or "chores" if that seems more appropriate.) If you are a "list-maker," write down your normal "to-do" list:

____

____

____

____

Which are your favorite?______________________________________

Which are your least favorite?_________________________________

____

____

____

(Notice that I gave more space for your least favorites.)

Now, I have a challenge for you:

Take this "least favorite" list and show it to Jesus. Ask Him to give you His perspective on "activities" on this list. Let Him open your eyes to see what He sees.

He was so good to me when my kids were preschoolers. He always reminded me that what I was doing—changing diapers, wiping noses, picking up toys, etc—had eternal value. He was so sweet to encourage me when I was knee-deep in dirty diapers that I was serving Him by serving my kids. He gave me His eternal perspective on being a stay-at-home mom. If anyone needs an eternal perspective, it is a stay-at-home mom. If this is you, be encouraged dear one, He is right in the middle of it with you. He wants to let you see things from His eyes.

One day, I was in the "thick" of things, at home with two toddlers. I was feeling lonely and bored with my routine. I was sitting in my rocking chair, trying to comfort the little one that was crying in my lap, as tears fell down my face as well. I just cried out to Jesus. "I'm lonely. I'm bored. I'm tired." Jesus is so tender. He wiped the tears from my face and said, "My precious child, you are not alone. I am right here with you. I am right here listening when they cry. I am right here laughing when they do something so cute. I love watching them play, watching them learn, watching you love them. I am right here walking through this motherhood thing with you. In fact, I gave it to you as a gift. Let me show you this season of your life through My Eyes. It will change how you see all the tasks you do every day. It will put a little "bounce" in your step. I am holding your hand as you hold theirs."

Is that the sweetest thing you have ever heard? My perspective got shifted that day … from the temporary to the eternal … from the insignificant to the purposeful … from myself to my Master.

Will you let Him do the same for you? He wants to let you look through His Eyes and He has perfect Vision.

How is He changing your perspective right now? ______________________________

____

DAY FOUR: PART OF THE FAMILY

Are you one of the lucky girls that got to grow up with an older brother? I wasn't, but I always wanted one. Someone to look out for you, protect you, punch out high school boyfriends for you—you know the kind. I had girlfriends who had big brothers. I thought they were so cool. They would drive us places before we were able to drive ourselves; they were the seniors when we were freshmen; the "coolest" guys at school.

God didn't see fit to give me a big brother. Maybe I was too much to look out for so God just had to look out for me Himself. (I gave my parents a little trouble as a teen.) I guess I just always wanted someone to count on to "take up" for me, come to my rescue. I was the oldest child so I didn't have an older sibling to defend me. (Not that I was good about defending my little sister … I was the one picking on her.) Did you know that even though I don't have an earthly "big brother," I do have a heavenly Big Brother. He watches out for me, defends me, and comes to my rescue. He is on my side. He is even "cooler" than those senior guys in high school. He is bigger and tougher. He stands in front of me and says, "If you're messin' with her, you're messin' with Me." (Makes me want to look over His shoulder at the one "picking" on me and stick out my tongue.)

Do you need someone to defend you? Have you been hurt lately? He wants to come to your rescue, to be your Defender. He will "take up" for you.

How do I know? Let me show you what the Bible says about Jesus, our Defender.

Read the following Scriptures and answer the questions:

Psalm 35:23 What does David (writer of this psalm) ask the Lord to do?____

Exodus 14:14 What will the Lord do for you? ____________________________

What do you need to do?____

Deuteronomy 1:30 Where does the Lord go? a) before us b) behind us c) beside us

Nehemiah 4:20 Our God _________ fight for us.

Did you write a great big "WILL" in the blank of the last statement? Our God WILL fight for us. It doesn't say He "might" or He "won't" or He's "too busy". His Word says He will fight for us.

In what area(s) of your life do you need Him to "fight" for you?

____

____

____

____

Don't you just hate a tattle-tale? I never wanted to be labeled one at school so I usually kept my mouth shut. Nobody likes a tattle-tale. But sometimes, don't you wish you had someone to tattle to? Someone whose eyes wouldn't roll as you talk about your woes? Well, let me tell you a little secret. Shhh. Just between you and me. I tattle to Jesus all the time. I tell Him when someone hurts my feelings, or when someone was rude to me, or when someone left me out, or when someone didn't appreciate something I did for him or her. I run and tell Jesus on them. Guess who I tell on the most. My husband. Not because he's a bad person; in fact, he's a wonderful man. I thank God for him all the time (whenever I'm not tattling on him). I guess it's because my husband is the person closest to me, the one who is around me the most, so he has the most opportunity to "hurt" me. I used to let my tongue go crazy when I would get mad at him for something. I can raise my voice with the best of them. I can also say hurtful things that I have to apologize for later. I'm not saying that I never get mad and raise my voice anymore, but, more often than not, I just run and tattle" to Jesus. I tell on my husband to Jesus. Sometimes, I sense Him saying, "I'll take care of it." Other times, I sense Him saying, "Let's think about what caused this reaction." (His nice way of reminding me that I started it.) Other times, He might allow me to see the situation through my husband's eyes. Whatever the response, I know He doesn't mind me running to Him. In fact, He wants me to.

When He tells me that He'll take care of it, He really does. I think my husband is starting to figure out that I'm tattling on him. The last few times that he has hurt my feelings (he doesn't usually mean to), he has come home from work and said something like, "I've been feeling so convicted today. God showed me how I hurt your feelings and I'm really sorry." Wow. I didn't even have to nag him about it.

My point is … if you don't have a big brother, don't worry. Jesus wants to watch out for you. If you do have one, let Jesus watch out for you anyway. Give your brother a break.

Let's close today by writing a prayer to Jesus.

Write a prayer asking Him to defend you, or thanking Him for taking up for you recently, whatever is on your heart:____

DAY FIVE: BEEN THERE, DONE THAT

All this week, we've been talking about the Humanity of Jesus. Like I said before, I think it's harder to wrap our minds around this than His Deity. I like to imagine God creating the universe, hanging the moon and the stars, setting the boundaries for the oceans, designing each leaf on every tree. What is harder for me to imagine is God, becoming a human being, and living among the rest of us. What if your next-door neighbor was God? Would you keep your yard cleaned up a little better? Would you make sure your dog did not "go" in His yard? Would you be willing to get His mail while He's gone? What kind of mail do you think He would get in His mailbox? Latest sports magazine? Christian magazines? Probably no bills since He already owns everything. It's just hard to think about God living among us. But that is exactly what He did over 2000 years ago. He became human and lived with other people … people just like you and me.

He started life just like we all did, as a baby in our birthday suits. He went through the toddler stage. I guess He wasn't a "terrible two" since He did no wrong. He grew up with the kids on His street, probably played a few games of kick-ball or something like that. He also went through the tumultuous teenage years. Do you think He had acne? My husband says teenage girls are lucky because at least they can wear make-up to cover acne. Teenage boys are just out of luck when it comes to that. Jesus became a "grown up" as well. He walked on this earth for 33 years. I would say He experienced a lot of the same things that you and I have experienced in life. No, He never went to a drive-in movie, but He did do some things similar to us. He went to work, to church, to dinner parties, to weddings and to funerals. He visited friends. He went on trips.

We have a Friend, Jesus, who relates to us. He's not just the "Big Guy in the Sky" looking down on us, casually observing us like we are a bunch of ants Ever heard the saying that you don't know what it's like to be someone else until you've walked in their shoes? Well, Jesus walked in our shoes.

Let me show you from His Word.

Look up the following Scriptures and rewrite them in your own words in the space provided:

WHO is This?

John 1:14

____

____

Luke 2:52 ____

____

John 6:42 ____

____

Mark 6:3 ____

____

____

Mark 1:35 ____

____

Mark 4:38a ____

____

Mark 10:16 ____

____

John 2:2 ____

____

John 21:9-13 ____

____

Did anything jump out at you in these verses? Did anything surprise you? Write down your thoughts.

____

____

____

____

Did you notice that Jesus even cooked breakfast? Now that's my kind of Guy. I like any man who is willing to cook. Did you notice that Jesus had a job (other than coming to save the world)? He was a carpenter. He must have been a nice Guy because He got invited to weddings and dinner parties. He must have really loved children too. I bet He even volunteered for nursery duty. Do you see that Jesus lived a life a lot like ours? It makes me feel better to know that I have a Friend Who understands what I'm experiencing in life—the good and the bad. One of my favorite verses in Scripture is found in Hebrews.

Fill in the blanks:

Hebrews 4:15 "For we do not have a High Priest Who is unable to ____________ with our weaknesses, be we have One Who has been tempted in every _______, just as we are---yet was without sin."

Don't you just love that? Jesus knows how we feel. He knows how it feels to be sad, to be happy, to be disappointed, to be lonely, to be busy, to be tired, to work, to have fun, to need a break. Isn't it nice to have SomeOne to talk to Who totally understands you and how you feel? He can be your very Best Friend. Just think. You and Jesus … BFF.

What do you really need to talk to a friend about right now? Take some time and talk with Jesus. He is a great Listener.

WEEK THREE:

OMNIPOTENT KING

"For in Christ all the fullness of the Deity lives in bodily form, and you have been given fullness in Christ, Who is the head over every power and authority."

Colossians 2:9-10

DAY ONE: CHEERS

DAY TWO: HUNGRY PEOPLE

DAY THREE: BAD WEATHER

DAY FOUR: 'GOLD'FISH

DAY FIVE: 20/20 VISION

DAY ONE: CHEERS

I hope you enjoyed spending some quality time with your Friend last week. He's a down to earth kind of Guy. Make no mistake, however. He is no ordinary Friend. Last week, I enjoyed pondering the ordinary things Jesus experienced in His life on earth. I am really excited about this week because we are going to look at some extraordinary things Jesus did.

Have you seen anything extraordinary lately? What comes to mind when you hear the word 'extraordinary'? ____

____

____

____

I'm thinking mind-blowing, unbelievable, incomprehensible ... just to name a few. These words describe our Lord. He is Extraordinary.

Let's look at the first recorded miracle that Jesus performed.

Read John 2:1-11.

Where was Jesus in this story? ____________________________________

Who asked Him for help? ____

What was the need? ____

How did Jesus meet the need? ____________________________________

Extraordinary. Jesus took ordinary water and turned it into extraordinary wine.

Remember the shoebox I mentioned in week one? I've tried, more than a few times, to take an ordinary, plain shoebox and transform it into something extraordinary. I've already told you how unsuccessful I have been in the project area. You see, God is good at projects. He specializes in transforming the ordinary into the extraordinary.

You and I are kind of like an ordinary, plain shoebox until God gets a hold of us. He does amazing things we could not have even imagined, unexpected things, mind-blowing things.

Let me tell you something extraordinary God did in the life of my husband. He is no ordinary man. Everyone who meets him, loves him. (Sometimes I get mad because I think everyone likes him better than they like me.) He is so much fun and he just loves life more than anyone I know. God took a little, ordinary business idea and transformed it into something extraordinary. When we were in our early 20s, my husband told me that he was to start a lawn-mowing business. Now, this was a little odd to me because we didn't even own a lawn mower. We were newly married and were living in a rented duplex … so we didn't take care of our own lawn. My husband had no business degree, no business experience, didn't even know anyone personally who owned their own business. It was a long shot, but my husband felt that God had laid this on his heart so he went for it. He started out with a little red truck, a used mower, and a borrowed weed-eater. The rest is history. Today, 15 years later, my husband is a well-respected, successful owner of a large landscaping/snow removal company. You don't mind if I brag on my husband a bit, do you? But I brag most about my Lord. He took this ordinary idea, this young man with no business experience and no money and He did the amazing, the extraordinary. I am amazed more and more each day. I am so proud of my husband who has worked harder than anyone I know, but he will tell you Who the glory goes to. You know the One … Jesus.

What is something ordinary that you could give to Jesus and let Him do the extraordinary?

____

____

____

Has He done the extraordinary in your life lately? If so, how?

____

WHO is This?

____

____

____

____

____

____

Spend some time thanking Him for all the amazing things He has done.

DAY TWO: HUNGRY PEOPLE

You know what sounds good to me right now? Mexican food. I wish you and I could go to lunch today at my favorite Mexican restaurant. The best part is the chips and salsa they bring you before the main course. I always tell myself that I won't eat too many chips because I want to save room for the main course. But the chips are so good and I'm always so hungry when I go there. It's not like I don't end up having room anyway for the main course. Nothing satisfies your hunger like a big plate of Mexican food.

While we're talking about food, let me tell you about some people who were hungry … and there was no Mexican restaurant nearby.

Matthew 14:13-21, Mark 6:30-44, Luke 9:10-17, John 6:1-15.

Answer the following questions:

Where and when does this story take place? ________________________

How large was the crowd? ________________________

What was the dilemma? ________________________

How much food did the disciples find? ________________________

What did Jesus do? ________________________

____

How does the scripture describe the people after they ate? ________________

____

This was a huge crowd of hungry people. Can you imagine trying to feed 5,000 people? I have enough trouble trying to feed my family of five. Jesus had no trouble at all. He fed all those people and they were **satisfied.**

Look up the word "satisfied" in a dictionary and write what you find: ____

____

WHO is This?

____

Would you describe yourself as "satisfied"? ____________________________

____

Is there something that you continually "hunger" for in your life? ______________

____

____

____

Jesus longs to satisfy your hunger. He knows exactly what you need. He has what will satisfy your craving.

During each of my pregnancies, I craved chocolate. I sent my husband out many times for anything chocolate. I remember sitting down in front of the TV one night and eating an entire package of Oreos. I'm not talking about an individual pack like you buy at a gas station. I'm talking about the family pack with 3 rows of cookies.

With my first son, I got on this kick of boxed chocolate cake mix. I would make a cake…my husband would eat one piece…and I would eat the rest. I had to satisfy my chocolate craving. I still crave chocolate every now and then. I sometimes want it so badly that I get in my car and drive to the grocery store just to buy a Hershey Bar. I sit in my car, eat it, and then I'm satisfied.

Let's look up some Scriptures about satisfaction.

Fill in the blanks:

Isaiah 55:2 "Why spend money on what is not bread, and your labor on what does not ____________? Listen, listen to Me, and eat what is good, and your soul will ____________ in the richest of fare."

Psalm 63:5 "My ________ will be ____________ as with the richest of foods; with singing lips, my mouth will praise You."

Psalm 103:5 "Who __________ your __________ with good things so that your youth is renewed like the eagle's."

Psalm 107:9 "For he ____________ the thirsty and ________ the hungry with good things."

Luke 6:21 "Blessed are you who __________now, for you will be _________."

Let's close today by bringing our needs to Jesus. He longs to satisfy our needs with good things. Talk with Him about what you are longing for, what you desire, what you've been missing. He is the Great Satisfier. He will give you things that are even better than chocolate.

Write down any thoughts.____

____

____

____

____

____

____

____

DAY THREE: BAD WEATHER

Do you like a good thunderstorm? I do, as long as it's not a dangerous one that might do some harm. There's nothing like staying in the house in your pj's, curled up with a good book or a good movie. I love to lie in bed at night and listen to a storm, under the covers where I'm all warm and safe. I usually am not alone for long as all three kids and the dog end up in the bed with my husband and me. But it's kind of cozy, isn't it? What I don't like are the storms you actually have to take extra measures to find safety in. Those aren't as much fun because fear becomes factor. Have you ever been in a storm that caused you to be afraid?

If you asked my mom and dad about their scariest moment, they would tell you about the time a tornado "visited" their neighborhood. They were both at home, just minding their own business, when the weather took a turn for the worse. The sky darkened, the wind picked up, then the local TV station declared a tornado warning. You always think it will hit anywhere but your own house, don't you? I think my parents thought this as well. But it came right through their backyard. When they realized it was headed toward their neighborhood, they decided to seek safety. Since they live in a ranch with no basement, the safest place is the hallway closet in the center of the house. It's hard to picture them huddled up together in this tiny closet. They both say that the house shook and sounded like a train was driving right through the house. They couldn't even hear the prayers they were saying out loud. The Lord was with them that day and kept them safe, thank goodness, as well as most of the house. They just had a few insignificant repairs to make. They both say that they will never forget that storm and the fear it brought with it.

I know SomeOne else Who has been in a bad storm. His Name is Jesus.

Read Matthew 8:23-27.

Where is Jesus in this story? ______________________________

What is He doing? ______________________________

What are the disciples doing? ______________________________

How does Jesus "handle" the storm? ______________________________

What was the result? ______________________________

Describe the reaction of the disciples: ____

____

____

What about you? Is there a "storm" in your life right now? Is it bringing fear along with it? Jesus has the power and authority over any and every storm. Talk with Him about your storm; admit your fear to Him. He may calm your storm immediately, or He may allow you to walk through it with Him by your side. I cannot say what His sovereign purposes are for your life concerning your storm. But what I do know for sure is that He wants to calm **you** in the midst of your storm. Will you let Him?

Write a prayer to Him today: ____

____

____

____

____

____

____

____

____

DAY FOUR: 'GOLD' FISH

Are you getting more and more excited about Jesus as we move through this study? I'm so excited about Him I can hardly stand it. Just this week alone, we've seen Him do the extraordinary, satisfy the hungry, calm a crazy storm, and we haven't even gotten through Week Three.

Today, I want us to look at another story in Matthew, another amazing story with Jesus doing amazing things.

Read Matthew 17:24-27.

Did you see another thing Jesus has in common with us? He had to pay taxes. Can you imagine? The Owner of the entire universe had to pay taxes. Well, I guess He didn't have to, but He chose to. Maybe He didn't want the IRS coming to His house … so He paid His taxes.

What did He tell Peter to do? ____

____

____

How did Jesus seem about paying taxes?

a)A little worried b)extremely anxious c)almost in tears d)not one bit worried

Did you notice that Jesus wasn't a bit worried about how He was going to pay His taxes? I wish I could say the same. Since my husband owns his own business, tax time can be a little scary. April 15th is not our favorite day of the year.

Do you know why Jesus wasn't worried? Because He is Owner of all things. All things belong to Him. That house you live in belongs to Him. That car you drive belongs to Him. That closet full of clothes belongs to Him. Those children you are raising belong to Him. Everything we have is just on loan because it all belongs to Him. Do you think those people on the rich-and-famous shows know that they don't really own their stuff? But when you know Who Jesus Is, you know Who really owns everything.

Let's do some deductive reasoning.

If Jesus owns everything and we are His most precious creation and He cares about us more than anything else, then we should never have to worry about any provisions because He will provide whatever we need.

Read the following Scriptures and choose the best answer.

What does God do concerning the poor? Psalm 68:10

a)Forgets them b)Tells them to "come back later" c)Laughs at them d)Provides for them

What does He provide for those who fear Him? Psalm 111:5

a)Rain check b)Pat on the back c)Plaque with your name on it d)Food

What does He provide for His people in the desert? Isaiah 43:20

a)Heat lamp b)Sand-blower c)Mirage d)Water

What does He provide for the naked? Ezekiel 18:7

a)Hair dryer b)Cologne c)2 tickets to ballet d)Clothing

What will He provide for those who are tempted to sin? 1 Corinthians 10:13

a) "Get out of jail free" card b)Wooden paddle c)Coffin d)A way out

What does He provide those who put their hope in Him? 1 Timothy 6:17

a)Only what we can pay back b)Only what we deserve c)Everything

I hope you had a good laugh with some of those answers. I meant them to be humorous. But my point is more serious. Do you see Jesus as your Provider? He wants to provide for all your needs. He doesn't want you to worry about anything. He owns the world and wants to give it to you.

WHO is This?

What do you need to ask Him for today? ______________________________

____

____

____

How can you show that you trust Him for this provision? _______________

____

____

____

Will you thank Him in advance for this provision? Write a prayer:

____

____

____

____

____

____

Watch and see what He will do.

DAY FIVE: 20/20 VISION

I'm not one of those people blessed with perfect vision. I started wearing glasses in the third grade, although I probably needed them before that. I just didn't realize I couldn't see perfectly. People from the health department would come to school every year and do eye exams. They figured out that I didn't have perfect vision, I needed glasses. I wore glasses until 8th grade, when I moved up in the world and got contact lenses. I kept my glasses for the times when I had to take a break from the contacts. My husband says my glasses were so thick that I could see into the future. (He knew me in junior high.) When I became an adult, I started hearing about this thing called LASIK surgery. I heard that people who had worn glasses their entire lives were coming out with 20/20 vision. It had to be a miracle. I couldn't imagine not needing glasses, being able to see the clock when you wake up in the morning, not having to reach for those glasses. Wow. I couldn't remember ever being able to see perfectly without glasses. On my 30th birthday, as my birthday present, my husband took me to have the surgery. I was pretty nervous having anything done to my eyes. They make you sign a paper saying you won't sue if you end up blind. I let them perform the surgery on me. I tell everyone it's the best thing I have ever done, besides asking Jesus in my heart, marrying my husband, and having my three kids of course. So I guess it's number four on my top 10 list. It's been several years now, but I still can't believe it. I have vision that's even better than 20/20, which I didn't even know was possible. Last time I was in for an eye exam, I had 20/15 vision. I should be able to see through walls with that kind of score.

I know SomeOne else Who has perfect vision. In fact, His vision is more than perfect. We don't know what He would score on an eye exam, but I bet His score would blow the minds of those giving the exam. He would probably read the letters on the chart and then proceed to read the letters on the chart in the next room and the ones down the hall and the ones in the office down the street. In fact, He might read the letters on the chart in the next country. I know He wouldn't be prescribed any glasses, not even the thick ones (remember mine?), because He doesn't need them to see into the future. He already knows the future. He created the future ahead of time.

Let me show you some exciting verses from Isaiah.

Read Isaiah 42:8-9, 44:6-8, 44:24-28, 45:11-12, 45:21, 46:9-11.

WHO is This?

Is your mind reeling from what you saw in these verses? This Jesus, that we have spent so much time with over the past few weeks, knows what our future holds. He knows everything that our paths will encounter. How amazing is that? We can talk to the One Who knows everything before it happens. He has perfect vision.

How is your vision? Is it a little cloudy? Is it a little near-sighted? Do you have trouble seeing in the dark? Don't worry. Jesus wants to let you see through His Perfect Eyes. He wants to show you your circumstances through His eyes. He wants you to see your suffering in a new Light. He wants to let you see His Hand at work. All we have to do is ask Him.

What, in your life, do you need Jesus to shed some Light on? ____________________

____

____

____

____

There was a time when I really needed to look through His eyes. My middle son had a lot of difficulty starting out in elementary school. He had some learning difficulties and some developmental delays. We took him to a specialist to have him tested for learning disabilities, etc. My husband and I had to attend a follow-up appointment to hear the results of this testing. Most of it was hard to hear because I didn't like the results and wanted a "do-over." We were told, "He'll never do this, he'll never do that, he'll always struggle with this, he'll probably not get to do that …." I was more than a little discouraged. I came home from that meeting and didn't know quite what to do with the information I had just received. I immediately ran to the Lord and fell on my face before Him. I cried out to Him with heart-felt tears. I asked Him, "What do I do with this information? How am I supposed to deal with this? How do I help my child? I need to see this from Your Perspective." The Lord was so sweet in His answer to me. He led me to Psalm 139.

Read Psalm 139.

I had read this passage many times before and even had some of it memorized. But God asked me to do something I hadn't thought of before. He asked me to read it out loud putting my son's name in it. Talk about perspective. Tears flowed down my face as I read that passage aloud, speaking my son's name with every verse. God showed my son to me through His Eyes. This took all the worry from me and answered the questions I had just asked. God will take care of my child. He knows him and knows his future. He holds my son in His hands.

Today, my son is a successful fifth grader. I was so pleased with his most recent report card. God is amazing. He has done mighty things in my son's life and I have had a front row seat.

Spend time asking Him to give you His Perspective on your present circumstances. Take a look through His Eyes. I think you'll be amazed at what you see. Let Him do some LASIK surgery on your eyes … I bet your vision will be better than 20/20.

WEEK FOUR:

SERVANT TO ALL

"Who being in very nature God, did not consider equality something to be grasped, but made himself nothing, taking the very nature of a servant, being made in human likeness."

Philippians 2:6-7

DAY ONE: ABC'S AND 123'S

DAY TWO: HOUSE CALL

DAY THREE: HANGING OUT

DAY FOUR: SPECIAL TOUCH

DAY FIVE: DIRTY FEET

DAY ONE: ABC'S AND 123'S

Do you remember who taught you the ABC's? Who taught you to write your name? Who was your favorite teacher in elementary school? There is usually one we never forget. My third grade teacher was really special. She had a sweet, soft voice that you could just sit and listen to all day. (I guess that is a good thing since I did have to sit and listen all day at school.) She was so nice, I couldn't wait to get to school every day. She never raised her voice or embarrassed anyone. Our class was never afraid to ask questions or make mistakes because she had such a loving way about her. She loved her class and loved watching us learn.

Describe your favorite teacher. ____

____

____

____

Jesus did a lot of teaching. The Gospels are filled with accounts about Jesus teaching. He taught individuals, small groups, and huge crowds. He taught highly educated people, uneducated people. He taught in the synagogue, in homes, on the hillsides. He even taught in a boat. He was always teaching the people around Him.

Let's take a look at Jesus, the Teacher according to the Gospel of Mark.

Read Mark 1:21-22, Mark 4:1-2, Mark 6:6b, Mark 6:34, Mark 9:30-31a, Mark 10:1.

Jesus was a busy Man. He was constantly taking opportunities to teach those around Him.

What reason does Mark 6:34 give for Jesus teaching the crowd? ________________

____

Don't you just love it? Jesus had compassion on the crowd. He saw them as "sheep without a shepherd." That is exactly what we are without Jesus, sheep without a Shepherd. Sheep without a shepherd to guide them spend most of their time just wandering around. They don't know which way to go on their own. They walk right into danger. They get lost from the rest of the flock. They don't know when it's time to come home to the safety of the pen. They are hopeless without a shepherd to guide them.

Do you feel like you are just wandering around spiritually? Are you intimidated by Bible Study? Have you tried to read the Bible before and just didn't understand any of it? Do you avoid spiritual discussions for fear of sounding dumb? Well, you are in luck. I know this great Teacher Who knows everything about the Bible. He would love for you to be His student. He doesn't charge much … in fact, He does it for free. He just requires a little of your time. He will sit down with you as you open your Bible. He will show you things you've never seen before. He will explain the meaning of those verses that are hard to understand. He will even show you how to apply the verses you are reading to your present circumstances. He loves to see His child's eyes light up as He teaches His Truths to them.

I help with a lot of homework at my house. I usually sit down with each child, one on one, and help them with whatever they are having trouble with, which usually ends up being math, which just happens to be my specialty. Math was my college major so I actually enjoy helping my kids with math. I have to suffer through the rest of the subjects with them, but not math. I guess I love to teach what I know.

Jesus loves to teach what He knows. And guess what, He knows everything. There is no subject beyond His understanding. All we have to do is ask Him to teach us. If you need help handling your finances, Jesus is a great Financial Advisor. If you need help learning a new job, Jesus is a wonderful On-the-Job Trainer. If you need to know how to handle your children, Jesus is the Perfect Parent. If you need to know how to make some changes, Jesus is great at Restructuring. If you need help bringing order from chaos, Jesus is the Best Organizer.

What do you want Him to teach you? In what areas of your life could you use a little direction?

Make a list.

We'll call it our "Help Needed" list.

____

____

____

WHO is This?

____

____

Fill in the blanks:

James 1:5 "If any of you lacks wisdom, he should ________ God, who gives generously to _______ without finding fault, and it will be _________ to him."

All we have to do is ask. Give your "Help Needed" list to Him and ask for help. Trust me. He will become your favorite Teacher.

DAY TWO: HOUSE CALL

One of my favorite shows growing up was "Little House on the Prairie." I watched it every day after school. My sister and I would even "play" the show when we weren't watching it. I always wanted to be Laura because she was my favorite character. As a kid, one thing I thought was neat, was that no one ever went to the doctor in their town. The "Doc," as he was called on the show, came to your house if you were sick. You didn't even have to get out of bed, get dressed, and head into town in your buggy. "Doc" would come right to your house, right to your bedroom and give you a diagnosis, and hopefully, some medicine to make you feel better. He didn't get paid in the typical manner either. He went home with payment in the form of a chicken or a basket of eggs or an apple pie.

I doubt you or anyone you know has ever received a house call from a doctor, unless you heard stories from your great-grandma. I guess house calls are a thing of the past. I sure wish doctors had been doing house calls when my kids were babies. There is nothing worse than having to get a sick baby dressed, bundled up, and out the door. Except maybe getting a sick baby out the door with a toddler in tow as well. I always dreaded the doctor visits when the kids were younger. I even dreaded the "well" visits. It was the parking garage I didn't like. It was always full so I would drive around in endless circles until a parking space opened up....which would usually end up being the space that was the farthest away from my destination. After parking the car, I would proceed to get my children out of the car. (This was no easy feat.) Once I would get everyone in the door, I was ready for a nap. Why didn't they do house calls when my kids were babies? It would have been so much easier.

Jesus made many house calls. The Gospels record more than a few house calls that Jesus made. Let's look at some of them together.

Read Matthew 8:14-15.

Whose house did Jesus enter? ________________________________

Who was sick? ____

What did Jesus do for this sick person? __________________________

Read Matthew 9:18-26.

WHO is This?

Whose house did Jesus enter? ______________________________

Who was "sick"? ______________________________

What did Jesus do? ______________________________

Can you imagine Jesus making a 'house call' to your house because you were a little "under the weather"? Guess what? He hasn't really changed with the times. He still makes house calls. You can call Him anytime and he'll be right over. You don't have to worry about getting dressed, bundled up, or having to start the car. Jesus will meet you right where you are. You don't have to go looking for Him. He will come to you. That's my kind of doctor. He will tell you what your ailment is and give you just the right medicine. His diagnoses are always correct and He never gives the wrong medicine. He has never even had a malpractice suit filed against Him.

Do you have an "ailment" for Him to tend to? ______________________________

____

____

____

Why don't you call the Doctor right now? He'll be right over. Let Him give you His medicine. I know you will start feeling better right away.

"For I am the Lord Who heals you." Exodus 15:26

DAY THREE: HANGING OUT

Who do you like hanging out with? Your husband? A neighbor? An old friend? A new friend? Girls in your "Moms Club"? A coworker?

Write down some names that come to mind: ______________________________

____

____

____

Why do you like hanging out with these particular people? ____________________

____

____

____

I bet your reasons **didn't** include: because they are boring, don't like to do anything fun, are always negative, always try to tell you what to do, are always critical, never laugh at your jokes, never crack a smile, like to watch paint dry, always talk about themselves, always interrupt you, never let you pick where to go eat, always find something wrong with everything.

For some reason, I'm guessing that these words **don't** describe the people on your above list. Am I right?

My list probably looks a lot like your list. I have my husband, who is tons of fun. I have several girl friends I like "hanging" with. I like hanging out with my mom and my sister. I even wrote my dog on the list because I like hanging out with her. She lets me do all the talking.

You know SomeOne else Who is at the top of my list? Jesus. I love hanging out with Jesus. He is a ton of fun. He likes the same stuff I do. He often lets me pick what I want to do. He laughs at my jokes. He makes me feel like I'm fun to hang out with too.

WHO is This?

Does this surprise you? Did you think Jesus would be boring? Wouldn't know a fun time if it snuck up on Him? Doesn't like to laugh? Was weaned on a pickle? You know the type. The one who tries to keep everyone else from having a good time.

I'll tell you for sure. This is not the Jesus that I know. He loves to just hang out and have some fun.

Read Mark 2:15.

What does this verse say Jesus was doing with the sinners and tax collectors at Levi's house?

a)Teaching them b)Rebuking them c)Offering advice to them d)Having dinner with them

Read Matthew 26:6-7.

What does this verse say Jesus was doing while at the table?

a)Complaining about the food b)Talking with His mouth full c)Hogging the conversation d)Reclining

Read John 2:1-2.

What reason does verse two give for Jesus attending the wedding?

a)His mother made Him go b)He loved wedding cake c)It was an excuse to buy a new pair of sandals d)He was invited

It sounds like Jesus was a Guy people liked to hang out with. He got invited to dinners, people stayed to hang out around the table after dinner with Him, he was on the guest list at weddings. He must have been fun to be around.

Just recently, I got to spend a whole day with Jesus. It was more like a day and a half. Jesus and I had a sleepover. My husband was taking care of the kids so I could have a break. I needed one. We have a little place to stay at a lake that is not far from home. I decided to go there for an overnight stay and I invited Jesus to come too. We had the best time. We enjoyed sitting on the dock, in the sun, looking out over the water. We took a nap in the hammock on the back porch. We sat on the porch swing and watched the sun go down. We even worked a 300-piece jigsaw puzzle. We watched a movie and ate my favorite snack, chips and salsa. We had a great time.

During that sleepover, He wasn't really teaching me, giving me advice, correcting me, or training me. He was just hanging out with me.

Would you like to hang out with Jesus? I know He wants to hang out with you. He's just waiting for an invitation.

I challenge you to set a date to hang out with Jesus. It doesn't have to be an overnight getaway. In fact, you don't even have to leave your house. Just pick a time that you can do something with Him. Go for a walk together, sit on your back porch and have lemonade, go shopping together, go get ice cream, whatever you like to do. I'm sure He will like it too.

After your getaway, come back to this lesson and write down your experience.

____

____

____

____

____

____

____

____

____

DAY FOUR: SPECIAL TOUCH

You've heard the expression "… just needs a woman's touch." My husband was recently describing a friend's bachelor pad to me. He said it needed a woman's touch. I could already picture it before he described it to me—white walls, no color anywhere, mismatched furniture, hodge-podge decorations. (This is what happens when there is no woman in the picture.) Women just have that special touch. We can turn a house into a home. We can make each room inviting. There's a warmth that a woman brings to a home.

My father-in-law knows this first-hand. He was a bachelor for many years, until he met a certain woman. She flipped his house upside down, but in a good way. She came in, transformed this uninhabitable house and made it a lovely home. I couldn't believe it. She painted, tore out walls, threw out furniture. She did everything short of bulldozing the house and starting over. The finished product was proof that a woman just has a special way about her, to make things lovely, to add color and warmth, to make things beautiful.

I don't know many men who have this touch, but I do know One. He has that special touch that makes thing lovelier, more beautiful, more colorful, more inviting. I bet you already guessed Who. It's Jesus.

There's something about Jesus' Touch.

"He who looks at the earth, and it trembles, who touches the mountains, and they smoke." Psalm 104:32

Read Matthew 8:3.

Who did Jesus touch? ______________________________

What was the result of His touch? ______________________________

____

Read Matthew 8:15.

Who did Jesus touch? ______________________________

What was the result of His touch? ______________________________

____

Read Mark 7:33-35.

Who did Jesus touch? ____

What was the result of His touch? ____________________________________

____

Read Luke 7:14-15.

Who did Jesus touch? ____

What was the result of His touch? ____________________________________

____

Read Mark 10:13-16.

Why were the people bringing children to Jesus?

a)To have Him babysit b)To have Him teach them to be good c)To have Him spank them d)To have Him touch them

Wow. Jesus has an amazing touch. He can reach out and touch someone and make them clean, make them whole, make them well, make them alive, make them free. He can pour blessings on them.

Where do you need a touch from Jesus? _______________________________

____

____

____

____

WHO is This?

His amazing touch can heal a wound, break down a wall, take away a grudge, heal a broken heart, revive a buried dream, instill hope in a hopeless situation, mend a relationship, take away a bad habit, breathe life into a dying marriage.

Take time right now to ask Him to touch you where you need it most.

DAY FIVE: DIRTY FEET

One of the most vivid portrayals of Jesus as a Servant is found in John's Gospel.

Read John 13:1-10.

Describe the scene of this story. ______________________________

____

____

Describe Jesus actions: ______________________________

____

____

____

What was Peter's initial reaction? ______________________________

____

What was Jesus' answer to Peter in verse 8? Fill in the blanks:

"Unless I ______ you, you have ___ _______ with me."

I don't know about you, but I would get a little grossed out if I had to wash a bunch of grown men's feet. I think women have "cute" feet. I love to have a pedicure and get my toes painted. Have you seen all the designs they will do on your big toe? I got a little crazy one day and had them paint flowers on my big toes. It turned out so cute, I went around showing everyone my feet. But the word 'cute' doesn't really come to mind when I think of men's feet. One of the times I went to get a pedicure, the place was full of women. A man walked in and asked for a pedicure. You could've heard a pin drop. I felt bad because everyone stared at the guy. Now, let me just say, there is nothing wrong with a guy treating himself to a nice pedicure. But since it took awhile for the nail professionals (all women) to decide who was going to be assigned to him, I don't think any of them were excited about doing his pedicure. Just my observation, of course.

WHO is This?

Maybe I shouldn't be grossed out by men's feet (no offense to any men that might be reading this), but there is something that all of us should be grossed out by—our sin.

Our sin is gross. It makes us dirty. It makes us stink. It makes us "not so cute." It makes us ugly. It should make us want to "jump in the tub".

What does James 1:15 say about sin? ____

____

Did you notice from John 13 that Jesus told Peter that he could have no part of Jesus unless Peter allowed Jesus to wash him?

This is true for us too. Our sin separates us from God. The only Person Who can wash away our sin is Jesus. After He washes us clean, we are no longer separated from God. We can have a real relationship … a personal relationship … a one on one relationship … with Almighty God.

"But now in Christ Jesus, you who were once far away have now been brought near through the blood of Christ." Ephesians 2:13

Have you asked Jesus to "wash you clean"… to forgive your sins? He is willing. You can "jump in His tub".

If you haven't asked Jesus to be your Savior and Lord and to forgive your sin, and you are ready to do so, turn to the back of this study and read "Steps To Salvation." If you pray the prayer written in that section, tell someone, a pastor, a friend, a family member, so they can celebrate with you. I would love to celebrate with you too. Send me a note, if you like. You'll find my contact information in the back of the book.

If you know Jesus as Savior and Lord, do you have any unconfessed sin in your life that you need to talk with Him about right now?

Spend some time in prayer.

WEEK FIVE:

SEATED AT GOD'S RIGHT HAND

"After he had provided purification for sins, he sat down at the Right Hand of the Majesty in heaven."

Hebrews 1:3b

DAY ONE: BACK STAGE PASS

DAY TWO: RED CARPET

DAY THREE: PREFERRED SEATING

DAY FOUR: PAPARAZZI

DAY FIVE: THE CROWN GOES TO …

DAY ONE: BACK STAGE PASS

Have you ever been to a concert and had a back-stage pass? If so, lucky you. If not, try to imagine what it would be like to have a back stage pass to a concert featuring your favorite artist. Wouldn't you be so excited? I'm sure you would love the concert, but the best part would be afterward. You would get to go behind the stage and enter into the artist's personal space, where not many people get to go. You would see the person in a different light, in a more intimate setting. You would meet the artist personally, face to face. How cool would that be? You would probably even get an autographed CD.

Did you know that Jesus has a back-stage pass to the Throne Room of heaven?

Let's use our imaginations for a few minutes. Try to imagine what this throne room looks like? Let your imagination run wild. Write your description of Heaven's Throne Room. ____

____

____

____

____

____

Scripture gives us some "snapshots" of this Room.

Let's look at a chapter in the last book of the Bible.

Read Revelation 4.

Describe this Throne Room according to Revelation 4: ____________________

____

____

Kind of mind-blowing isn't it? Sure beats back stage at a concert. Jesus goes in the throne room anytime He wants. Scripture tells us He is there right now, sitting at the Father's Right Hand. He hangs out with the Father all the time.

Did you know that you and I can go into the Throne Room of the Almighty God too? As long as we're with Jesus. He takes us by the hand and walks right in there with us. He says, "She's with Me" and no one questions it. We are just as welcome there as He is.

Read Hebrews 4:16. Fill in the blanks:

"Let us then _______________ the throne of grace with _______________, so that we may receive mercy and find grace to help us in our time of need."

Did you see that? We don't have to be afraid to go into the Throne Room because we're with Jesus. We just point at Him and say, 'I'm with Him'... and walk on in, no questions asked. We can enter into the Holy Presence of God Almighty because of Jesus. He made it possible for us to approach God. It is unfathomable.

Will you take time to enter into the Throne Room now and worship the One Who sits on the Throne?

Here are a few Scriptures to help you worship:

Revelation 4:8, 4:11, 5:12, 5:13, 7:10, 7:12, 15:3-4

DAY TWO: RED CARPET

Have you ever had the red carpet rolled out for you? I have. Well, it was sort of pretend, but it still involved red carpet. We planned a special morning for our MOPS group at church. (MOPS stands for Mothers of Preschoolers.) We decided to call it a "Morning with the Stars." We wanted the moms to feel special so we rolled out the red carpet, literally. Everyone pulled out an old evening gown and came to MOPS like stars. We had the red carpet at the entrance as everyone came in, we even had a photographer snapping pictures. I think the women really enjoyed being treated like royalty. Most of us never get the red carpet rolled out for us.

Did you know that heaven rolls out the red carpet for Jesus? It is an even bigger deal than the Emmy's or Oscar's. Thousands upon thousands of angels show up to welcome Jesus onto the red carpet. Even all of creation bows to worship Him.

We are going to spend some time looking at Psalm 148. I want you to imagine all the angels and all of creation rolling out the 'red carpet' for Jesus as you read this Psalm.

Read this Psalm once silently, letting it sink in. Then read it again aloud.

I think you will find this passage even more amazing as you hear yourself speaking the words.

Make a list of everyone and everything that is to praise the Lord according to this passage. ____

____

____

____

____

Do you have a long list? Are you in awe of our Lord? All of creation rolls out the red carpet for Jesus in heaven and on earth. Do you know why?

Because He is **Worthy.** He is Creator of All Things. He is the Author of Life. He is the King of Kings. He is the Lord of Lords. He is Majestic. He is Above All Things.

He is All-Knowing. He is All-Powerful. He is Eternal. He is the Beginning and the End. He is the Great I Am.

He is the King of Glory.

How has your thinking toward Jesus changed since the beginning of this study?

Will you end today in prayer thanking Him for revealing more of Himself to you?

DAY THREE: PREFERRED SEATING

My husband and I took our kids to Disney World this year over Christmas break. I wouldn't recommend going this time of year. It seemed as if all of North America was there that week. If you were there too, I am not surprised. We had a good time seeing everything, we just didn't spend a lot of time doing anything. The lines for everything were just too long. The Magic Kingdom closed the gates every day that week by 10 a.m. because the park had reached capacity. It took us 1 ½ hours to get from the parking lot to the entrance to the park. We were in for the crowd of our lives. At least they tell you how long the wait is going to be in each line, so you are not caught by surprise as you wait two hours for a ride. After seeing the wait time for each ride, we told our kids, that each ride "didn't look like that much fun." We just mostly walked around and ate lots of food.

They did offer something called "Preferred Seating" to some of their shows. You could purchase a special ticket to a show and not have to get in line over an hour before the show starts to get a seat. They actually reserve a seat for you in the "Preferred Seating" section and you can show up 5 minutes before the show starts. We didn't know about this of course, until we went to a show, stood in line for a long time, and watched all the "Preferred Seating" people walk in and sit right down front as the show was starting. We were in the back fighting to save seats for the rest of our group. People get a little irritated when you try to save a whole row of seats.

Did you notice the verse on the front page of Week Five?

Where does Hebrews 1:3b say that Jesus is seated? ______________________________

____

Now that is what I call "Preferred Seating". It doesn't get any better than that. I thought the "Preferred Seating" section at an amusement park was cool, but it doesn't even compare to the "section" in which Jesus sits in heaven.

Let's look at some other verses that speak about this special seat.

Luke 22:69   Ephesians 1:20-21   Colossians 3:1

What do you learn about Christ's position in heaven from these verses?

____

____

____

Let me show you something even more unbelievable.

Fill in the blanks:

Ephesians 2:6 "And God raised us up with Christ and ____________ us ________ him in the heavenly realms in Christ Jesus."

Did you see what that verse said? We have "Preferred Seating" in heaven. We get to sit with Jesus. Can you believe it? We don't even have to buy a ticket. Jesus already paid for our seat and He is saving it for us. He won't let anyone sit in our spot.

Spend some time thanking the One Who saves your seat.

DAY FOUR: PAPARAZZI

Do you know anyone famous? I mean, personally? Someone who can't go out in public without be "mobbed" by a crowd? Someone who can't go shopping, out to dinner, to see a movie, or even blow his or her nose without drawing a crowd? I sort of feel bad for those people. Notice how I said 'sort of,' because they always have people following them around. You see proof of it in the "star" magazines. Picture after picture of famous people going about their business. Here's one celebrity taking the dog for a walk, another talking on the cell phone, another getting in the car, another drinking coffee. They aren't usually doing anything exciting. They just draw a crowd because of who they are. People will run to take a picture of a famous person picking his or her nose, just because of the celebrity status.

I know SomeOne, personally, Who is famous. He always draws a crowd. You wouldn't believe how many people run to meet Him. He is more famous than Elvis. You've heard of Him. Jesus.

Let's look at some Scripture about the crowds that followed Jesus. He couldn't go anywhere without drawing a crowd. People wanted to see Jesus, to hear Him speak, to witness His miracles, to watch Him in His daily life.

Describe the scenes in the following passages:

Matthew 14:13-14 ____

____

____

Mark 2:1-4 ____

____

____

Mark 3:7-10 ____

____

____

Mark 5:21-32 ______________________________

____

____

Luke 8:19-21 ______________________________

____

____

John 6:22-24 ______________________________

____

____

Jesus drew crowd after crowd after crowd. Crowds of thousands. Crowds that "pressed in" to get closer to Him. Crowds that followed Him from town to town. Relentless crowds, excited crowds, desperate crowds, curious crowds, forceful crowds, all trying to see Jesus.

Let's look at one more "crowd" account.

Read Matthew 21:1-11.

Describe the scene. ______________________________

____

____

____

____

WHO is This?

I love verse 10. "When Jesus entered Jerusalem, the whole city was stirred and asked, 'Who is this?'"

What is your answer? ____

____

____

____

____

____

DAY FIVE: THE CROWN GOES TO ...

What is it about girls and crowns? Every little girl dreams of wearing a crown. When my daughter was younger, she loved to wear costumes. Her favorite ones were the princess costumes because she got to wear a crown. She would prance around the house and demand "honor" from the rest of the family.

I have never seen so many little girls wearing crowns as I saw on our Disney trip. Everywhere you looked, there were sparkles, jewels, glitter on top of each little head. There must be something about wearing a crown. The girls didn't just walk, they strutted, they held their heads up high (I guess so the crowns wouldn't fall off), they curtsied, they drew attention. They expected 'royal' treatment.

If you have never worn a crown, no need to worry. There will be a time for you to wear one.

Read the following Scriptures and fill in the blanks:

1 Corinthians 9:25 "Everyone who competes in the games goes into strict training. They do it to get a ___________ that will not last; but we do it to get a ____________ that will last ____________."

2 Timothy 4:8 "Now there is in store for me the _____________ of righteousness, which the Lord, the righteous Judge, will ___________ to me on that day—and not only to me, but also to all who have longed for his appearing."

James 1:12 "Blessed is the man who perseveres under trial, because when he has stood the test, he will receive the _____________ of life that God has _______________ to those who love him."

1 Peter 5:4 "And when the Chief Shepherd appears, you will receive the ___________ of glory that will never ___________ away."

WHO is This?

Are you excited about your crown? I bet it will be beautiful. All 'sparkly,' 'glittery,' 'shiny.' I bet you will look great in it. You might even feel like 'prancing around' in it. You will probably feel like royalty. You will be royalty. Your crown will be all your own. You won't have to share it with anyone, won't have to worry about anyone taking it away, won't have to pass it on to the next winner. You will be able to keep it forever.

You don't ever have to give it away, unless, of course, you wanted to, but why would you want to? It's yours. Who would you possibly want to give it to? Your neighbor? Your co-worker? Your mother-in-law? Surely not. Before you decide whether you'll keep it forever, let's look at some more Scriptures.

Read Revelation 4:4-11.

What do the 'elders' do with their crowns? ____

____

We might wear our crowns proudly at first, but when we see Jesus, we will fall down and lay our crowns at His feet.

Let's end today by reading Revelation 19:11-16 and ponder the question … Who Is This King of Glory?

WEEK SIX:

SAVIOR ON A CROSS

"But they shouted, 'Take him away. Take him away. Crucify him!' ... Pilate handed him over to be crucified."

John 19:15-16

DAY ONE: FEAR

DAY TWO: SLAVERY

DAY THREE: DARKNESS

DAY FOUR: SEPARATION

DAY FIVE: DEATH

DAY ONE: FEAR

Can you believe this is our final week together in this study? I have so enjoyed introducing you to the truth about Jesus Christ. If you have just met Him through this study, I count it the highest honor to have introduced you to Jesus. If you have come to know Him better through this study, I praise God that He allowed me to part of your journey. I pray that you will continue seeking Him through prayer and Bible study.

I have looked forward to this week's lesson with great anticipation. This is the climax of our study. We have seen Jesus our Creator, Jesus our Friend, Jesus our Servant, Jesus our King. But have you met Jesus our Savior?

My husband ran into a friend the other day. He knew she hadn't been going to church anywhere so he invited her to come to church with us. She immediately began to share her negative feelings about church. She said she was so tired of going to church and having everyone tell her that she needed to "get saved." She then looked at my husband and very passionately said, "Saved from what?"

Maybe you have that very same question. Why would you ever look for a Savior if you don't realize your need to "be saved"? This week, I want us to look at what Jesus came to save us from. You might be surprised. You may find yourself running to your Savior.

Did you know that Jesus came to save us from FEAR? Notice I spelled it with all caps, because fear can be pretty BIG.

What are you afraid of? Make a list of your top fears. ______________________________

____

____

____

Do you know what my greatest fear used to be not that long ago? Public speaking. I feared it worse than death. I would've taken a bullet to the head rather than get up in front of a group of people and have to say anything. I couldn't even say my name if I had an audience of more than five. I used to avoid, at all cost, any situation that might put me in front of an audience. I began developing this "social anxiety" (as they call it today) around the age of 13. I almost didn't survive my high school speech class. As an adult, my fear didn't go away, it only grew. I wouldn't even speak up in my Sunday School class of 20 people because I didn't like to have all eyes on me.

Do you know what God did? He put me in a ministry that involved nothing but speaking to an audience. Can you imagine? He put me right in the middle of what I fear most. He pulled me out of my comfort zone and helped me face my fear. It was a long process with what I call "baby steps" but by the end of my time in that ministry, I couldn't wait to get my hands on a microphone. I had stuff to say. I wanted to share what Jesus was doing in my life and I wanted to encourage other women on their spiritual journey. Let me share one of my favorite verses about fear.

Psalm 34:4 "I sought the Lord and he answered me; he delivered me from all my ____________."

I love that verse because that is exactly what He did for me. I am a living testimony for that verse.

Christ came to save us from our fears. We don't have to let fear take over us. Jesus is greater than our fears. Let's see what God's Word says about fear.

Write the following Scriptures in your own words:

Psalm 23:4 ____

____

____

Psalm 27:1 ____

____

____

WHO is This?

Psalm 46:1-3 ____

____

____

____

Psalm 112:7-8 ____

____

____

Isaiah 41:10 ____

____

____

Isaiah 43:1-2 ____

____

____

____

So then, what shall we fear? Tomorrow? Bad news? Hard times? Sickness? Those who wish us harm? War? Job loss? Death?

Jesus came to set us free from fear. We don't have to fear anything. Jesus has everything under control. Did you know that nothing 'surprises' Him? He has your entire future in His Hands.

Remember the song we would sing as children, 'He's Got The Whole World In His Hands'? Why would you need to worry? He's got YOUR whole world in His Hands.

Give your list of fears to Jesus right now. Ask Him to set you free from your fears.

"In this world you will have trouble. But take heart. I have overcome the world."

John 16:33b

DAY TWO: SLAVERY

Have you ever felt like a slave? If you are a mother, then I bet you answered 'yes.' I know I often feel like I'm a slave to my children. Just this week, two of my three children have been sick and home from school. To top it off, my husband hurt his back and has been home from work for a couple of days. Talk about slavery. My days have been filled with, "Mom, I need this," "Mom, I need that," "Honey, could you get me this?", "Honey, would you mind getting that?", "Mom … Mom … Mom." I fluffed pillows, straightened blankets, made chicken soup, fixed milkshakes, bought medicine, found movies, poured hot chocolate, made a few hundred trips up and down the steps, and none of it was for me. I was serving my family—wholeheartedly, of course.

Maybe you've felt that way before, about your job, your ministry, or whatever it is that demands a lot of you.

Did you know that you are a slave to sin, apart from Christ? Every one of us is born as a slave to sin. What is sin? Sin is anything we do that displeases God. It is all the things we do that we shouldn't do, as well as all the things we don't do that we should do. Apart from Christ, we are helpless when it comes to our sin. We just can't get it together. No matter how hard we try, we always fall short. We keep making the same mistakes over and over. We just can't keep ourselves out of trouble. It's because sin controls us.

Let me tell you about this guy named Paul who wrote about his struggle with sin. See if this sounds like a familiar struggle.

Read Romans 7:14-25.

Describe Paul's struggle. ____

____

____

Did you feel exasperated for him as you read his struggle? Did the struggle sound familiar to you? Have you been in Paul's shoes? We all have.

Who can rescue us from slavery to sin, according to verses 24-25?

____

Hallelujah. Jesus Christ our Lord. He came to release us from our slavery to sin. He broke sin's power over us. We don't have to continue walking in sin, we are free to choose not to sin. Yes, we will all still mess up from time to time, maybe even every day, but we have the power (in Christ) to choose not to sin. We can overcome it. Let me show you.

Fill in the blanks:

Romans 6:2 "We died to ______; how can we ________ in it any longer?"

Romans 6:4 "We were therefore buried with him through baptism into death in order that, just as Christ was raised from the dead through the glory of the Father, we, too, may live a ________ life."

Romans 6:6 "For we know that our old self was crucified with him so that the body of ________ might be done away with, that we should no longer be ___________ to sin."

Romans 6:11 "In the same way, count yourselves __________ to sin but __________ to God in Christ Jesus."

Romans 8:9a "You, however, are controlled not by the ________ _______ but by the Spirit, if the Spirit of God lives in you."

Are you feeling relieved? We don't have to struggle with sin on our own. Christ died to free us from sin's hold over us. We have His power to overcome our sin. We don't have to keep making the same mistakes over again. We can rely on Christ's power to set us free?

What sin(s) are you struggling with in your life right now? ______________________

Will you lay them at the feet of Jesus and let Him set you free?

DAY THREE: DARKNESS

Isn't everything scarier in the dark? For example, if I asked you to walk through the cemetery with me today at noon, would you go? But what if I said I needed to go at midnight instead? Now that's a different story. I bet you could come up with many excuses not to go, other than it would be past your bedtime.

I went to a slumber party at a friend's house when I was in 8th grade. Her house was right next to a cemetery. During the daylight hours of her party, no one thought much about the cemetery, but when the sun went down, we all got a little spooked. We played a game of 'truth or dare' out in her back yard. Most of the dares had to do with the cemetery. I was dared to run and touch one of the graves (all alone) and then run back. I could've won a gold medal in the Olympics that night, I ran as fast as lightning.

There's just something about darkness. It's funny how my kids change when the sun goes down. Suddenly, they don't want to go in the basement all alone, or out to the mailbox to get the mail, or upstairs to get something when the lights are all off. I always have to go upstairs and turn the lights on so they'll go up and get ready for bed.

Can you imagine if we had to live our entire lives in the dark? Without ever having any light? That is exactly what life is like apart from Christ. It is entirely in the dark.

Write the following verses:

Isaiah 50:10 ____

____

____

____

Psalm 107:14 ____

____

____

WHO is This?

Isaiah 9:2 ____

____

____

Isaiah 42:16 ____

____

____

____

Isaiah 60:2a ____

____

Isaiah 61:1b ____

____

____

Read John 8:12.

Who is the Light of the world? ______________________________

Who will never walk in darkness? ______________________________

Dictionary.com defines 'darkness' as: the absence of light; wickedness or evil; obscurity, concealment; lack of knowledge or enlightenment; lack of sight, blindness.

What areas of 'darkness' do you need Jesus to shed His light on? ________________

____

____

If you are following Jesus, you don't have to walk in darkness. He is the Light that enables you to see. You don't have to grope around in the dark. He wants to 'light up' your entire life.

"You, oh Lord, keep my lamp burning;

My God turns my darkness into light."

Psalm 18:28

DAY FOUR: SEPARATION

My middle son had a bad case of separation anxiety when he was younger. He was the one you could hear crying in the nursery at church (from outside the building). He wasn't the one who cried when he was first dropped off and then stopped. He was the one who cried the entire time he was away from me. I was the one the nursery workers were least excited to see before church and most excited to see after church. My son continued to have this separation anxiety even in early elementary school. I was the mom you would see trying to 'drag' a child down the school hallway. When he was in kindergarten, I would walk him to his classroom, help him hang up his coat and backpack, and then tell him good-bye. This was not a quick process. He would hug me, then hug me again, and then hug me again, until I finally had to pull away or he would never get in the classroom. As I walked away, he would wave good-bye again and again. He wouldn't go into the classroom until I was out of sight. I could hear this little voice as I turned my back to him. It would break my heart. "'Bye Mom … love you Mom … bye Mom … see you real soon … love you Mom … bye …" Many days I left in tears because I knew how hard is was for him to be away from me as his mother.

Do you think God's heart broke when He had to separate from His most precious creation because of sin? I bet He had tears in His eyes as He had to walk out of the garden that day. Let's read the story.

Read Genesis 3.

What sin did Adam and Eve commit? ______________________________

____

What did they do when they heard the Lord coming? ____________________

____

List some consequences of their sin: ____________________________

____

____

____

What was the biggest consequence of their sin? ______________________________

____

When I read this story in Genesis, my heart breaks for Adam and Eve. You know they wished like anything that they could spit that apple out of their mouths and start over. But it was too late. They chose to sin. My heart not only breaks for them, but it breaks for God too. He must have been so sad to have to punish His children. I can't imagine how He must have felt to have to send them away. It must have been the worst day of His life.

You see, sin separates us from God because God is Holy. He cannot tolerate sin because of Who He is. Let me show you.

Read 1 Samuel 2:2, Psalm 24:3-4, Psalm 77:13, Psalm 99, Isaiah 6:1-5.

On our own, we cannot enter into the presence of a Holy God. We are sinners. We are unclean. We are separated from Him and there is nothing we can do to get to Him. But guess what? There is SomeOne Who made a way for us to come near to God. His Name if Jesus. He paid for our sin and erased it from our record so we could be holy and enter into the presence of a Holy God.

Ephesians 2:13 "But now in Christ Jesus you who were once _______ away have been brought __________ through the blood of Christ."

WHO is This?

Hebrews 10:10 "And by that will, we have been made _________ through the sacrifice of the body of Jesus Christ once for all."

Read Hebrews 10:19-22.

How can we enter the Most Holy Place?

a)very carefully b)shaking in our boots c)holding our breath d)with confidence

Who opened the way for us?

a)our neighbor b)our pastor c)the president d)Jesus Christ

We can ______________ God.

a)run away from b)stay at arm's length from c)look through the 'window' at d)draw near to

Can you believe it? Christ died on the cross to pay for our sin and make us holy so we could draw near to God Almighty—The Holy One. We would have been separated from Him forever. Talk about anxiety. I cannot imagine being separated from God with no hope of ever getting back to Him. But thank goodness for Jesus. He brought us back to God.

Have you accepted what Christ did for you on the cross? If not, turn to the back of this study and read the Steps to Salvation. Ask Him to open your heart today to see the price He paid for you.

Spend some time thanking Him for what He did for you.

DAY FIVE: DEATH

I cannot believe this is our last day together in this study. I have been so reminded of how Awesome my Lord is as I have written this study. I have literally fallen on my face before Him and just worshipped Him many times throughout this writing process. My God is Great.

I want to end this study by taking a look at the crucifixion of Jesus. I want you and I to stand at the foot of the cross together.

Read Matthew 26:36-27:54.

List ways that Jesus suffered on His way to the cross: ______________________________

____

____

____

____

Describe His death on the cross: ______________________________

____

____

____

____

____

Did you know that He died so you and I don't have to die? I don't mean that we won't die physically, I'm talking about spiritually. Those of us who know Jesus will spend eternity with Him. Our death on earth is just the beginning of our life in heaven with Jesus. This gives us a whole new perspective on physical death.

I had the privilege of holding my grandfather's hand as he left this world and entered eternity with Jesus. He had been sick for awhile. We knew he didn't have much longer so we tried to spend as much time with him as we could in his last days. I was sitting by his bed as he slept. His favorite gospel music was playing. I noticed his breathing slowed. I knew he was getting ready to leave us. I held his hand and told him to go be with Jesus. I was sad as I watched him take his last breath, but at the same time, I was bursting with joy. He was going to see Jesus face to face. He was going to meet His Savior in Person. He was stepping out of that old, sick body and into eternity with Jesus. That was the first time I had actually witnessed death firsthand. I thought it would be scary, but it was one of the most wonderful, peaceful, exciting experiences of my life. Thanks to Jesus.

Write these Scriptures:

John 3:16 ____

____

____

____

Romans 6:23 ____

____

____

1 John 2:25 ____

____

If we are in Christ, we are promised eternal life. This changes everything. If we knew that this world was all there is, how would we even get out of bed each morning?

Knowing what our future is allows us to live in the here and now with such hope. We have so much to look forward to. Let's end today with one of my favorite verses in the Bible:

"No eye has seen, no ear has heard, no mind has conceived what God has prepared for those who love him." 1 Corinthians 2:9

Remember the very first day of our study I asked the question, "Who do you say that Jesus is?" Write your answer to that question now that you have completed this study:

Who do you say that Jesus is? ______________________________

____

____

____

____

____

____

____

Conclusion:

My mom always tells a story about me when I was four. I was out in the back yard sitting under our weeping willow tree. She said that I sat there for the longest time. She watched me out the kitchen window, but after awhile, she went out to check on me. She walked out and asked me what I was doing, why was I just sitting under the tree for so long.

My reply brings tears to my eyes even today. I said, "I'm talking to God."

I don't even remember that day, but God was already drawing me to Himself. How precious.

When I was seven, I asked Jesus into my heart. I realized that He had died on the cross for my sin. I knew I wanted to go to heaven. I knew that Jesus loved me and I wanted to follow Him. I walked down to the front of my church and gave Him my heart.

He has been the Most Amazing Friend. He has walked with me every day of my life.

He has:

taught me,

protected me,

guided me,

encouraged me,

carried me,

strengthened me,

forgiven me,

surprised me,

laughed with me,

cried with me,

healed me,

helped me,

held me,

watched over me,

gone before me,

taken up for me,

blessed me,

uplifted me.

He is the most wonderful Person that I know.

My prayer is for you to seek Him daily and let Him show you more and more of Himself, and that you would fall more in love with Him each and every day.

Thanks for letting me share Him with you.

STEPS TO SALVATION:

1) Know that you are a sinner in need of a Savior.
   Romans 3:10-12 Romans 3:23

2) Know that the penalty for sin is death.
   Romans 6:23

3) Know that Christ paid the penalty for you.
   Romans 5:8

4) Know that salvation is a free gift.
   Ephesians 2:8-9

5) Accept this free gift.
   Romans 10:13 John 1:12

Dear Jesus,

I need you! I know that I am a sinner in need of a Savior. I know that my sin has separated me from You and apart from You there is no hope. I know that You are the Son of God Who died on the cross to pay for my sin. You made a way for me to come to You. I accept this free gift. I don't deserve it ... I can't earn it ... I just accept it as Your gift to me. Thank you for loving me enough to provide a way for me to spend eternity with You. I ask you to come into my life as my Savior and my Lord. I know You will never leave me or forsake me. I want to follow You the rest of my days. Amen

I would love to hear from you.

Visit my Web site:

www.CrystalTrower.com

If you would like to order additional books:

Go to www.christianpublish/bookstore.htm

or order from any local bookstore using ISBN #

If you prayed to receive Christ as your Savior and Lord during this study, please contact me so I can rejoice with you. Welcome to His family.

LaVergne, TN USA
13 March 2011
219922LV00001B/3/P

9 781603 832939